WILD AFRICA

ELEPHANTS

By Melissa Cole
Photographs by Tom and Pat Leeson

BLACKBIRCH®
PRESS

THOMSON
GALE

San Diego • Detroit • New York • San Francisco • Cleveland • New Haven, Conn. • Waterville, Maine • London • Munich

© 2002 by Blackbirch Press™. Blackbirch Press™ is an imprint of The Gale Group, Inc., a division of Thomson Learning, Inc.

Blackbirch Press™ and Thomson Learning™ are trademarks used herein under license.

For more information, contact
The Gale Group, Inc.
27500 Drake Rd.
Farmington Hills, MI 48331-3535
Or you can visit our Internet site at http://www.gale.com

Photo Credits: Cover © PhotoDisc; all photos © Tom and Pat Leeson Nature Wildlife Photography; except: back cover © CORBIS; page 3 © PhotoDisc

LIBRARY OF CONGRESS CATALOGING-IN-PUBLICATION DATA

Cole, Melissa S.
 Elephants / by Melissa S. Cole.
  p. cm. — (Wild Africa series)
 ISBN 1-56711-638-8 (hardback : alk. paper)
 1. Elephants—Juvenile literature. [1. Elephants.] I. Title.
 QL737.P98 C65 2003
 599.67—dc21
                                                    2002003225

Printed in China
10 9 8 7 6 5 4 3 2 1

Contents

Introduction

Elephants are one of the largest creatures on earth. They have stocky bodies, baggy skin, and long trunks.

An elephant's skin is baggy and wrinkled.

Elephants belong to a group of animals know as proboscids. This name comes from Greek words that mean "long snout."

Today, elephants are found only in Africa and Asia. African elephants make their home in central Africa, south of the Sahara desert. Most elephants live on grassy savannas and open woodlands.

Elephants have very long noses called trunks.

The Elephant's Body

Elephants are the largest land mammals on earth. The tallest known elephant was 13 feet (4 m) high at the shoulder—as tall as a one-story house! Male, or bull, elephants can weigh between 12,000 and 16,500 pounds (5.443 to 7.484 kg). Females, called cows, are usually smaller. They weigh half as much as males. Elephants can run at speeds of more than 20 miles (32.2 km) per hour when they are angry or frightened.

Elephant skin looks tough and leathery, but it is actually very sensitive. Elephants must coat their skin with dust or mud to protect it from sunburn, cuts, and insect bites.

An elephant coats its skin with water and mud.

This coating also helps elephants keep cool.

Most African elephants have giant teeth called tusks. Elephants use their tusks to dig for water or salt in the ground. They can turn over small trees with their tusks. They feed on the roots and tender leaves. Sometimes male elephants use their tusks as weapons.

Tusks are elephants' cutting teeth. Elephants grind and chew tons of vegetation each month. They use their 4 molars, or grinding teeth, to chew. Elephants grow 6 sets of teeth during their lifetimes. Each tooth can be more than a foot (30.5 cm) long and weigh 10 pounds (4.5 kg) or more.

An elephant can turn over a small tree with its tusks.

Special Features

One of an elephant's most amazing features is its trunk. The trunk is formed by an elephant's nose and upper lip, which are joined together. Trunks can weigh more than 300 pounds (136.1 kg). They contain more than 40,000 muscles and tendons, which allow them to twist and turn in many directions. Trunks are very strong. Elephants can use them to move trees. They can even help a fallen baby elephant get back on its feet!

Elephants have very strong trunks.

On the end of an elephant's trunk are flexible, finger-like parts. Elephants use them just as humans use their thumbs and forefingers. Elephants can pick fruit off trees, or pluck a single blade of grass from the ground.

An elephant uses its trunk to pick grass.

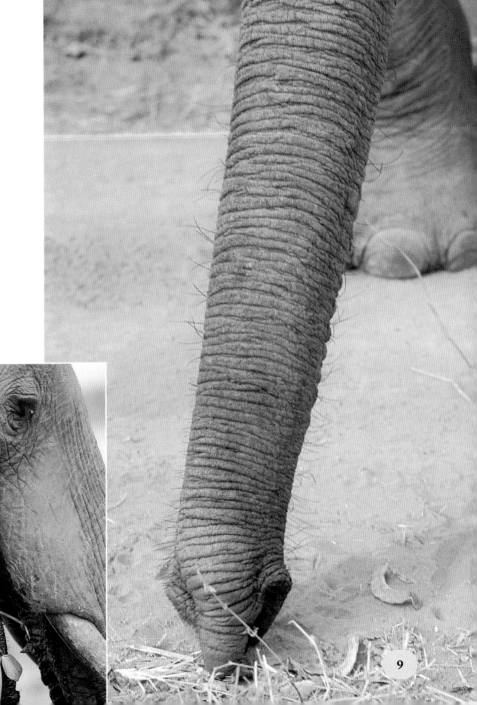

African elephants' nostrils are also at the end of their trunks. They have a good sense of smell. Elephants can smell something from as far as 5 miles (8 km) away.

A thirsty elephant can suck up as much as 2 1/2 gallons (9.5 liters) of water into its trunk at a time. It then places the end of its trunk into its mouth and squirts the water down its throat. Elephants also use their trunks like hoses to spray themselves and other elephants.

Elephants are good swimmers. An elephant can sink its whole body below the water's surface— with just its trunk sticking out like a snorkel!

An elephant sucks water into its trunk.

Because elephants have such huge heads, their eyes seem small. Each eye is protected by a set of 5-inch-(13 cm) long eyelashes. They keep dust and insects out of the eyes. When elephants swim, a special covering protects their eyes. Elephants do not have sharp eyesight. Their short necks make it difficult for them to turn their heads to look at something. Therefore, they rely more on their senses of smell and hearing than on their vision.

An African elephant's ears are larger than a bedsheet! An elephant flaps its ears when it is hot. Both ears have many blood vessels just beneath the surface of the thin skin. Fanning its ears cools the elephant's blood by as much as 10 degrees.

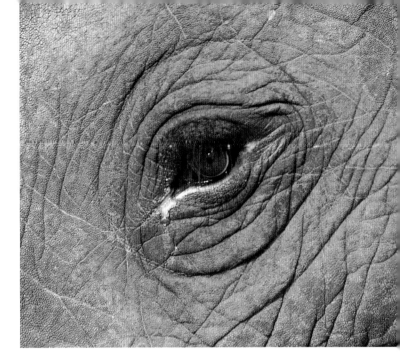

Top: A thin layer of skin protects elephants' eyes when they swim.
Bottom: Elephants flap their ears to cool down.

Social Life

Elephants are very intelligent, social animals. Female elephants live in family groups. A family group can have as few as 2 or 3 elephants, or more than 25. Females stay with the group into which they are born.

Usually the group's leader is the oldest female. She is called a matriarch. Cows usually do not become matriarchs until they are 40 to 50 years old. As cows grow up and have babies, called calves, the size of the group increases. If the group grows too large, some members may split up to form a new family group.

Family groups can have more than 25 elephants.

Unlike females, male calves leave their family groups when they are about 13 years old. Bulls may form herds of 20 to 100 animals or more. They travel together for a few days or weeks, but they do not form permanent groups as females do.

Elephants communicate with one another in many ways. In 1986, scientists discovered that elephants communicate using very low-pitched, or infrasonic, sounds. In open country, elephants can hear these infrasonic calls from up to 6 miles (9.7 km) away! Elephants use other noises to communicate when they are close to each other. They rumble or gurgle when they seem content. They screech and trumpet if they are angry or afraid.

Elephants have many ways to communicate with each other.

Smell and touch also are important forms of elephant communication. Elephants wrap their trunks together in a type of hug when they greet each other. They often place the tips of their trunks in another elephant's mouth to say "hello" or to offer comfort. Elephants often care for one another. They have been known to feed sick elephants. They can use their trunks to help injured family members walk.

Elephants seem to be interested in the skulls, bones, and tusks of dead elephants. They rub them with their trunks, or turn them over with their feet. Scientists think that elephants may be trying to identify the dead elephant.

Left: Elephants greet each other with a type of hug. **Right:** Elephants use their trunks to inspect the bones of dead elephants.

Feeding

Elephants are herbivores, or plant eaters. Elephants sometimes eat more than 300 pounds (136.1 kg) of food in a single day! They spend over 16 hours a day either eating or searching for food. Elephants also need plenty of water to survive. A full-grown elephant drinks between 30 to 50 gallons (113.6 to 189.3 liters) of water a day.

Elephants spend most of their day eating and looking for food.

Elephants eat more than 400 kinds of plants. In marshy areas, they feed on reeds and water plants. In wooded areas, they eat leaves, twigs, seedpods, bark, roots, and shrubs. Elephants seem to love fruit. They often will go out of their way to find figs, wild bananas, plums, and wild coffee berries. An elephant's height helps it to reach leaves and fruit in tall trees. Elephants can rest on their hind legs and reach their trunks up high—even higher than a giraffe is tall!

Elephants need salt and minerals in addition to food and water. Elephants search for salty soil or rocks and pick up pieces to suck on like candy. On Mount Elgon in Kenya, elephants go to a dark cave, called Kitum, to dig for salt. Scientists believe this cave, which is 525 feet (160 m) deep, 130 feet (39.6 m) wide, and 13 feet (3.9 m) high, was made by generations of elephants digging for salt over thousands of years.

Elephants can reach fruit in tall trees.

The Mating Game

▲▼▲▼▲▼▲▼▲▼▲▼▲▼▲▼▲▼▲▼▲▼▲▼▲▼▲

Although elephants can mate at any time, most elephants mate during the rainy season. Females are ready to mate when they are about 12 years old. Bull elephants also are ready to mate at this age, though they rarely get the chance to do so. Once young bulls begin to fight with each other or try to mate, older females chase them away from the family group. These young bulls then find a male group to join.

Females chase bulls away from the group once they start to fight.

A change occurs in bulls when they are about 25 years old. For 3 months a year, they go into a condition called musth (pronounced "must"). A small gland between each eye and ear swells. A dark, oily liquid drips from this gland and rolls down a bull's face. A bull in musth often fights other bulls for the right to mate with a female. During these fights, bulls can break tusks and sometimes even kill each other.

Males join family groups when females are ready to mate. Scientists have found that females call males with special infrasonic mating songs. When bulls hear these songs, they will come from far away to find a mate. After mating has occurred, bulls leave the family group. They do not help raise calves.

Bulls fight for the chance to mate with a female.

Raising Young

Females have a gestation period, or pregnancy, that lasts 18 to 22 months. An elephant usually gives birth to a single calf.

Calves weigh about 250 pounds (113.4 kg) and are 3 feet (1 m) tall at birth. Within 15 minutes of being born, a calf stands on its wobbly legs with the help of its mother's strong trunk. After a few hours, the calf begins to nurse. Calves curl their trunks out of the way to nurse.

It takes several years before a young elephant has complete control of its trunk. Often calves suck their trunks for comfort the way human babies suck their thumbs. They play with their trunks and wiggle them around until they get tired. Their trunks hang down in front. They often trip over them when they walk.

Calves nurse until they are 3 or 4 years old. When they are 6 months old, they start to eat plants. A calf learns which foods to eat by reaching into its mother's mouth to pull out a piece of whatever she is chewing.

Newborn elephants walk under their mothers to avoid the hot sun. This also offers protection from predators. Large predators, such as lions, leopards, and hyenas, prey upon lone elephants under 6 years of age.

Mother elephants care for their young for 10 years or more. They will often have another calf 2 to 3 years after the first one is born. When calves are 6 to 8 months old, they begin to play with other calves. Their games include running at each other, butting heads, chasing one another, and grabbing tails. These games help them learn coordination and social skills.

A mother elephant cares for her calf.

Elephants and Humans

In the 1800s, European hunters killed many elephants for their tusks, which are made of ivory. Ivory is used to make furniture. It is also carved into small objects. Killing elephants and selling ivory is now illegal in many countries. But the demand for ivory encourages poachers (illegal hunters) to kill elephants anyway. Helicopters and machine guns have made elephant hunting easier than ever before. This practice has increased over the last 40 years.

In 1990, there were an estimated 600,000 elephants living in Africa—in 1970, there were twice as many. People must protect elephant habitats and save these amazing, intelligent animals. Otherwise, it is possible that elephants will disappear within the next few decades.

People are trying to save elephants. African people are

People can help protect elephants from poachers.

beginning to realize that tourists are willing to pay money to see wild elephants in their natural habitats. Locals are able to earn a living as guides and park rangers instead of as ivory poachers. If this trend continues, elephants may continue to live long, peaceful lives on the African savannas.

Tourists enjoy seeing elephants in their natural habitat.

African Elephant Facts

Scientific Name: Loxodonta africana

Shoulder Height: 10–13 feet tall (3–4 m)

Body Length: 19–24 feet from head to tail (5.8–7.3 m)

Weight: Males weigh 12,000–16,500 pounds (5,443–7484 kg). Females are usually half that size.

Color: Dark gray

Reaches sexual maturity at: 12 years in both sexes

Gestation (pregnancy period): 18–22 months

Litter Size: Usually one calf at a time

Favorite Food: Leaves, grasses, bark, roots, seedpods, fruit

Range: Central Portion of Africa, South of the Sahara

Glossary

Gestation period The length of time that a female is pregnant

Infrasonic sounds Noises that are too low for humans to hear

Matriarch The female leader of a group—usually the grandmother or oldest female

Membrane A thin, protective layer of skin

Migrate To move from one area to another

Musth A condition that adult bull elephants go through once a year

Poach To illegally hunt an animal

Further Reading

Books

Dudley, Karen. *The Untamed World: Elephants.* Austin: Raintree Steck-Vaughn Publishers, 1997.

Levine, Stuart. *The Elephant.* San Diego: Lucent Books, 1998.

Taylor, Dave. *The Elephant and the Scrub Forest.* New York: Crabtree Publishing, 1990.

Patent, Dorothy H. *African Elephants (Giants of the Land).* New York: Holiday House, 1991.

Web sites

Oakland Zoo's Elephant Page
http://www.oaklandzoo.org/atoz/azeleph.html
Elephant Trust's Page
http://www.elephanttrust.org/
BBC Wildlife's Elephant Page
http://www.bbc.co.uk/nature/animals/wildfacts/elephants/fact_files/177.shtml

Index